GW00391916

The Great Brexit Cookbook
by Graham Hughes

Copyright © 2023

ISBN – 9781626133020

Library of Congress Control Number -
2022944006

Published by ATBOSH Media ltd.
Cleveland, Ohio, USA

www.atbosh.com

With thanks to Dave Critchley

FOREWORD
THE GLORIOUS TASTE OF SOVEREIGNTY

Now that we've put up massive trade barriers with our closest neighbours (as if we've just lost a major war) and rid our generous kingdom of them pesky *foreigners* who came over here and did all the jobs we didn't want to do, we are *finally* free to eat the godawful food of our once and glorious past.

However, many have forgotten how to cook cheap and tasteless dishes of low nutritional value such as stewed pigeon, nettle soup and boiled sheep's head.

This is where the *Great Brexit* Cookbook comes in.

I have discovered some wonderful old recipes for those that know their place: simpering under the jackboot of the neo-aristocracy.

This is my gift to working class morons and middle class graspers who go gooey-eyed and weak at the knees at the sound of a plummy voice and an expensive education.

May the miserable and restrictive future that they have voted to foist on their offspring taste as delicious as the dishes contained within.

> *N.B.– This is an advisory cookbook. While the recipes are real, your constitution might not match that of your syphilitic forefathers. The author takes no responsibility for injury, sickness, death, or economic devastation that may or may not arise as a direct or indirect consequence of preparation or consumption of the meals laid out in this august compendium.*

CONTENTS

SOUP *etc*. 9

PIGEON *etc*. 13

RABBIT *etc*. 25

KIDNEY DISHES 35

TONGUE DISHES 51

HEART & LIVER RECIPES 57

HEAD & BRAIN RECIPES 61

SAVOURY JELLIES 71

FRUITS OF THE SEA 77

MEATLESS DISHES 85

TASTY TREATS 93

BEVERAGES 103

DESSERT 107

About the Author 121

SOUP *etc.*

NETTLE SOUP

3½ pints stock
3½ pints young nettles
2 blades of chives, or little onion
6 tablespoonfuls of barley (or oat) flour
Salt and pepper to taste
A little sugar

Clean nettles, plunge in boiling salt water, and boil for 15 minutes. Pour away, and wash in fresh running water, cut up fine with chives, sprinkle with flour, then frizzle in a little fat. Add stock, boil gently in closed pan ¾ hour. Skim well, season, and serve.

N.B.—Poached eggs may be floating on top if desired to add nourishment.

BONE BROTH

5lbs. bones
4 carrots
1 onion
1 clove of garlic

Blanch bones in a metal pot by covering in cold water, bringing to the boil and simmering for no more than 15 mins. Drain and place bones and vegetables on separate trays in a hot oven for up to 45 mins.

Place bones and vegetables in a lidded metal pot, cover well with cold water and gently simmer for up to 24 hours. Strain the broth through a fine-mesh strainer. Reheat before serving.

N.B.—Knuckles, joints, feet and marrow bones work best.

GRUEL

Take of Robinson's patent groats 1 tablespoonful, mix with a wineglassful of cold water, gradually added, into a smooth paste; pour this into a stew-pan containing nearly a pint of boiling water, or milk, stir the gruel on the fire (while it boils) for 10 minutes; pour it into a basin, add a pinch of salt and a little butter, or, if more agreeable, some sugar, and a small quantity of spirits.

N.B.—When gruel is made for an invalid, butter had best be omitted.

PIGEON *etc.*

STEWED PIGEONS

3 pigeons
½ pint good stock
1 oz. butter
2 cloves
Small piece of parsley
½ tablespoonful flour
2 tablespoonsful sherry
Small onion

Cut the birds into four, fry in the butter, add stock, onion, cloves, and parsley, and simmer gently one hour. Mix flour with cold water; stir it into the gravy and boil. Dish up pigeons on a piece of fried bread, put gravy round and serve very hot. The parsley should be put in a little muslin, and taken out before consuming.

PIGEON (TO COOK)

Remove feathers and skin, cut off head and feet, clean, put in the body a piece of butter size of walnut, 2 teaspoonfuls of any sauce (H.P., O.K., etc.), a dash of pepper and salt. Make a good suet crust, roll out thin, place pigeon on it, with a thin slice of bacon on the breast, roll the crust over the bird to shape. Bake it and baste with bacon fat or butter. This makes the bird moist and of a pleasanter taste than is often obtained.

PIGEON PIE

Two or 3 pigeons, cut in half, a small piece of topside of beef, divided in cubes. Highly season with pepper and salt, sprinkle over with a tablespoonful of flour, put in a stew-pan with 1½ pints of cold water or stock. Simmer very gently till tender. Lay in a pie-dish, add 2 hard-boiled eggs cut in quarters. Reduce the liquid till it will just cover the meat, or if necessary add a little gravy. Cover the dish with nice pastry and ornament the centre with pigeon feet.

BRAISED PIGEON

Put 2 or 3 slices of fat bacon into a casserole, then a layer of sliced carrot, turnip, and a little celery; also a sprinkling of herbs; put in 1 or 2 pigeons, sprinkle with salt and pepper, brown in the oven, pour off any fat, add about 1½ pints of brown stock, cover and cook in oven very gently about 2½-3 hours. Baste occasionally. Serve cut in pieces in a casserole or whole on a dish with vegetables round.

ROAST PIGEONS

2 pigeons
1 oz. butter
1 oz. dripping
½ pint boiling water
2 tablespoonfuls good game gravy,
   or 1 of Liebig

Well flour pigeons, roll butter in, salt and pepper, put a piece into each bird's body. Bake in a sharp oven about 30 minutes, basting well with dripping. Add boiling water and gravy, thicken. Put each bird on a slice of toast, and pour gravy round. Serve with bread sauce and chopped potatoes.

WOOD PIGEONS (BRAISED)

Allow 2 slices of streaky bacon for each bird, put the bacon into a stew pan; put on this a split carrot, slice of turnip, and an onion slice, arranged flat. On this place the pigeons, add 2 tablespoonfuls water or gravy, cover with buttered paper and the pan lid, and cook gently 1½ hours, first quickly to brown, then very gently. Remove birds, brown tops under a grill or before a hot fire; strain the gravy, reduce by rapidly boiling, pour over the birds. Serve with browned crumbs and bread sauce.

ALBATROSS (TO ROAST)

After trussing, fasten on the breast a piece of fat bacon, tie up the feet in greased paper, put about 3 ozs. of dripping in a tin to get hot, put the bird in, baste at once. Cook 1 hour in hot oven, 10 minutes before serving baste and dredge over a little flour and finish cooking. Serve with fried croûtons of bread and brown sauce. Remove skewers, put in the tail feathers, garnish each end of dish with watercress.

ROOK PIE

Skin and draw rooks; be careful not to break the gall-bladder; divide birds into pieces, and soak in milk 2 hours; dry, season with salt and pepper. Arrange in dish with small pieces of steak, also seasoned; put in a few bits of butter, and cover with stock. Make a water paste of flour and water, bake gently 2 hours. When cold, remove the paste, fill up with stock, cover with puff pastry; bake in quick oven. Serve hot or cold.

SPARROW STEW

Truss 7-8 sparrows as for roasting, place in a
casserole or stew-pan, and about half cover
with fairly hot, slightly salted water. Cook
very gently by side of fire, or over small gas-
ring, keeping lid on. Drain and thicken and
brown liquid, and pour over it. May be
served with white onion sauce.

ROASTED SEAGULL

Let them hang for 3 or 4 weeks, dress and truss them; if the heads are left on they must be wrapped in greased paper to prevent burning. Sprinkle birds with pepper, salt, and flour. Place over the breasts a piece of fat bacon, cut in slits down centre to prevent curling. Put birds in dripping tin with little water and dripping; place in hot oven, baste well, let them brown nicely; add more water to prevent burning if necessary. Bake 1 hour. Serve with browned breadcrumbs, bread sauce, sausage, or bacon.

WOODCOCKS (TO SERVE)

Woodcocks should always be roasted, and placed on a slice of toast thickly spread with the trail, taken out after cooking. Baste very well with stock, garnish with lemon slices and sprigs of watercress, or with ribbon potatoes, nicely fried, and watercress laid on top of the birds. Woodcocks do not need the usual bread sauce and crumbs. A salad can be served with it if liked. Always cover the breast with bacon, unless cooked before the fire; 15 minutes is enough. Season the trail with lemon juice, pepper and salt, and cayenne, before placing on the toast.

RABBIT *etc.*

*N.B.—Do not catch, buy or poach
wild rabbits between February & August.*

A DELICIOUS WAY TO
COOK A RABBIT

Cut your rabbit into joints, wipe and dry. Take bread crumbs, mixed with chopped parsley, thyme, pepper, salt, and a little nutmeg. Put a layer of this mixture into a buttered dish, then a layer of rabbit, adding slices of bacon, and repeat again till the dish is full. Then fill your dish with milk and bake in a moderate oven till nicely browned.

RABBIT MOULD

Take 1 oz. of gelatine, soak all night till soft.
Joint a rabbit, and put it into a pan with
enough stock or water to cover. Add salt,
pepper, a few strips of lemon peel, and one
onion stuck with cloves. Stew gently till the
bones will separate from the meat. Take up
the rabbit, remove all the bones, strain the
gravy. Grease a mould, line it with two hard
boiled eggs cut in slices, fill with the rabbit
and cold boiled bacon or ham in alternate
layers. Put the gelatine in the gravy, and boil
till it is dissolved, season, and pour over the
meat in the mould. Let it stand till next day,
then turn out and serve.

RABBIT STEWED IN MILK

1 medium-sized rabbit
Quantity of milk
2 large onions
Seasonings
Bread crumbs

Cut up and flour the rabbit. Fry the onions in rings in low pan till quite brown, add the rabbit, bread crumbs, and seasonings then add enough milk to cover the rabbit. Simmer gently till tender, thicken the gravy, boil 10 minutes longer, and then serve. To be eaten either hot or cold.

GALANTINE OF RABBIT

2 lbs. veal
1 lb. sausages
¼ lb. bacon
1 hard boiled egg

Choose a nice square piece of rabbit, cut in half, and season thickly with pepper and salt. Take the sausage meat from skins, cut bacon in strips, and place in straight lines from top to bottom; cut the egg in quarters and lay it in. Again season well, then lay on the other half of the rabbit, and tie the whole in a pudding cloth, and boil gently for two hours. Add bones, carrot, turnip, and onions to saucepan. When boiled, untie cloth, and place between two dishes to press. When cold, trim the ends off and brush over with melted meat glaze. Serve on a lace paper, garnish with parsley.

RABBIT (STEWED) (1)

1 rabbit
¼ lb. bacon
Salt, pepper
3 cloves
2 onions
¼ pint milk

Split the head, soak with the neck in cold, salted water ½ hour, dry them; cut rabbit in nice servings and bacon in little pieces, place with seasonings in pan, cover with water or stock. Simmer 1½-2 hours, or till tender. Mix flour with milk, stir gently till it thickens.

RABBIT (STEWED) (2)

Cut rabbit in joints, roll in seasoned flour, fry till brown with an onion and 1 tablespoonful of dripping. Put into a stew-dish, with a piece of butter and little chopped ham; cover with stock or water, stew in oven about 3 hours; thicken gravy, and serve with sippets of toast, or make into a pic and serve hot or cold.

RABBIT AND MACARONI

Boil rabbit till tender, remove meat off the bones, cut in small pieces, mix with 1 oz. of boiled macaroni, 1 chopped onion, ½ pint of milk, salt, coralline pepper; simmer ½ hour, stir frequently. Just before serving, add 2 ozs. of grated cheese (optional).

HARE (JUGGED)

1 hare
2 onions stuck with cloves
A head of celery
2 carrots
Plenty of pepper and salt
Thick rasher of fat bacon
1 wineglass port wine
Butter and flour

Skin the hare, keep as much blood as possible with the liver and heart, cut in small pieces, and hare into neat joints. Melt a generous lump of butter in a frying-pan, fry the pieces of hare nice brown; put into a deep stew-pot with the blood, and cover with quite boiling water; add onions, cut up carrots, celery, and bacon in small pieces. Simmer in oven for 2½ hours. Put a piece of butter into a small pan with a tablespoonful of flour, stir till it browns, pour in some boiling liquor from the hare, stirring all the time, let it thicken, then pour into the stew-pot, adding the port; let it boil 5 minutes. Serve in a hot vegetable dish or tureen, with mashed potatoes.

RABBIT PUDDING

1 rabbit
1 onion
2 ozs. grated cheese
Suet or dripping crust
Salt and pepper

Stew rabbit and onion with a little stock, left-over gravy, or water, till tender. Line a basin with suet crust, fill with rabbit, and sprinkle in the cheese. Cover with crust. Steam 2 hours.

N.B.—May be put in a greased pie-dish and baked, or breadcrumbs used instead of the crust and baked. If the latter, add little bits of margarine over the crumbs, and sprinkle the top with browned crumbs. The rabbit may be fried brown in a little dripping if desired.

KIDNEY DISHES

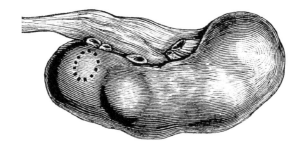

KIDNEY ENTRÉE OR SUPPER DISH

Slice thinly ½ lb. of ox kidney and ½ lb. of calf's liver, season with pepper and salt, and fry with a large onions, sliced. Meanwhile, grate up a large carrot and small turnip. Place all into a casserole or stewpan barely covered with hot water, cook slowly about 1¼ hours, or after 10 minutes' boiling it may be put into a hay-box for 3 hours; if so it will want reheating before the gravy thickening is added. Serve with mashed potatoes round.

RISSOLES OF KIDNEY

Kidneys
Lean ham
Bacon

Stew the kidneys in very little water till
tender. Take an equal quantity each of
kidney, ham and bacon; mince and season it,
and add a little chopped parsley and some of
the gravy. Roll out some pastry ¼-inch
thick, cut into squares, put some of the
kidney mixture on each, roll up, brush over
with egg and breadcrumbs and fry.

STEWED OX KIDNEY

Cut a fresh ox kidney into slices an eighth of an inch in thickness, soak for a few minutes in lukewarm water, drain and dry them thoroughly in a cloth, season with pepper, and dredge thickly with flour. Fry them in 3 ozs. of hot butter or dripping until nicely browned. Cover with cold water or stock, add a dessertspoonful of vinegar, a finely-minced eschalot, a tablespoonful of chopped parsley, a little salt and cayenne. Stew very gently for two hours; thicken the gravy, and add half-a-teaspoonful of mixed mustard before serving it.

OX CHEEK AND KIDNEY MOULD

Take one ox cheek, cut it up into dice, also one ox kidney, divide it down the middle and cut out the fat, then cut in fine slices, season, and cover with water, and stew 6 hours. Skim well and mould.

BEEF KIDNEY (1)

Trim and cut the kidney into slices, season them with salt and pepper, and dredge them well with flour, fry them on both sides and when thoroughly done lift them out, empty the pan and make gravy for them with a small slice of butter, a dessert spoonful of flour, pepper and salt, and a cup of boiling water. Shake these round and give them a minute's simmering. Add a little mushroom ketchup, lemon juice, eschalot, vinegar, or any sauce that will give a good flavour. Mixed herbs are to many tastes an improvement to this dish, to which a small quantity of onion shredded fine can be added if liked. 30 minutes to cook.

BEEF KIDNEY (2)

Slice the kidney rather thin, after having stripped off the skin and removed the fat. Season with pepper, salt, and grated nutmeg. Sprinkle over it plenty of chopped parsley or equal parts of parsley and eschalots chopped very small. Fry the slices over a brisk fire and, when nicely browned on both sides, stir in a teaspoonful of flour, and pour in by degrees a cup of gravy and a glass of white wine. Bring the sauce to the point of boiling, add a morsel of butter and a tablespoonful of lemon juice, and pour the whole into a hot dish, garnished with fried bread.

KIDNEYS (GRILLED) (1)

Stew sheep kidneys into a small pan with a little butter and water, with the lid on; when tender split open, season with pepper and salt, and grill quickly; thicken the gravy in the pan. Serve on toast or with bacon.

KIDNEYS (GRILLED) (2)

To prevent them going hard when grilled, divide kidneys in half, string a piece of fat bacon about the thickness of a match through, then steam for 5 minutes; afterwards grill in the ordinary way.

KIDNEY AND ONIONS
(STEWED)

One large Egyptian onion, about ½ lb., peel and cut in half, remove centre, lay in a sheep's kidney, a piece of butter, little pepper and salt, put one half on the top of the other, pin together with a thin wooden skewer. Put in a small basin or casserole with a little butter and water at the bottom of the basin. Cover with a plate or lid, and cook in a moderate oven not less than 2½ hours. This is a delicious supper dish.

KIDNEYS (STEWED)

4 sheep kidneys
½ small onion
1 oz. butter
3 teaspoonfuls flour
Pepper and salt

Cut kidneys in small pieces, roll in flour, chop onion fine; fry all together in butter until brown, add pepper and salt, and enough cold water to cover them; stew gently for 1 hour. Thicken the gravy a few minutes before serving.

KIDNEY OMELETTE

1 sheep's kidney
½ teaspoonful chopped parsley
2 eggs
Pepper and salt
½ oz. butter

Stew the kidney in a little gravy or water till tender, mince it; mix in the seasonings and egg yolks; then stir in lightly the whites, first well whisked. Melt the butter in an omelette pan, pour in the mixture; keep the edges loose with a knife; brown on the lower side; fold over, and serve immediately, keeping it out of a cold draught.

KIDNEY (SAVOURY)

One ox kidney, or half, according to size of dish required. Cut in thin slices; grease a pie-dish or casserole, put in alternate layers of sliced onion and kidney, season with pepper and salt, adding a little fat (goose or duck dripping is nice), pour over a little water, cover top with browned crumbs, place over it a lid or well-greased paper. Stew in the oven gently for 2-3 hours. Serve in same dish.

KIDNEY AND SWEETBREAD

1 lb. kidney
1 lb. sweetbread
1 egg
Breadcrumbs
Butter

Stew the kidney gently for 1 hour, then add the sweetbread, which has been steeped in hot water for 15 minutes. Stew together; then dip each piece in egg and cover with breadcrumbs, and fry in butter. Thicken the gravy, and flavour salt and pepper.

OX KIDNEY AND MACARONI

½ lb. kidney
4 ozs. macaroni
Pinch of allspice
Bay leaf and English mustard

Stew kidney in gravy in a casserole with spices for 1 hour, add macaroni broken in pieces, simmer 1 hour, or till all is tender. Serve in casserole.

KIDNEY TOAST

Prepare a couple of sheep's kidneys by removing the cores and skin, mince and cook them in a little brown gravy or stock for a few minutes, season, and add a little ketchup or mushroom sauce, and spread on toast; then put in the oven for a few minutes. Serve hot.

TONGUE DISHES

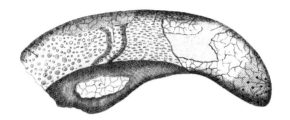

TONGUE SOUFFLÉ

1 large cup, cooked and minced tongue
1 small cup white sauce
1 teaspoonful parsley, chopped
Salt and pepper
3 eggs

Stir all together in a pan, adding beaten egg yolks the last. Cook 3 minutes, stirring all the time; cool, fold in the beaten whites of eggs. Put in a soufflé or pie-dish. Bake about ½ hour. Serve at once.

PICKLED TONGUES

6 quarts water
1 lb. salt
2 ozs. saltpetre
¼ lb. moist sugar

Boil together for 20 minutes; when nearly cold it will do for use. This will keep good for 2 months, and when skimmed and boiled up again with a little more salt it will be fit to use again.

Procure the tongue as fresh as possible; then rub the mixture well into all parts of it. Place in a flat bowl and cover with the mixture that is left, turn every day for 15 days, then boil slowly for 6 hours. This brine will keep for many weeks, and after taking the tongue out another might be dipped in without adding anything fresh.

OX TONGUE (TO CURE)

¼ lb. salt

2 ozs. moist brown sugar

½ oz. saltpetre

Mix together, and lay on the tongue, which should be in a deep dish to catch the liquor. Rub well, and turn over daily from 2 to 3 weeks. Allow to boil 1 hour for each pound.

Let it stand in the liquor till nearly cold, then remove skin and bones, put into a round deep dish, cover with a plate, and weight it down well.

N.B.—This quantity is for a tongue weighing 3-4 lbs.

TONGUE TOAST

Mince some scraps of cold boiled tongue, season with black pepper, stir in the beaten yolk of an egg, one to each breakfastcup of mince; add a little milk or cream. Heat well, and pour it over some slices of hot buttered toast.

HEART & LIVER
RECIPES

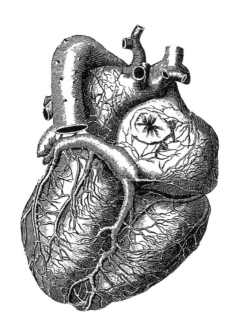

CALF'S LIVER (BAKED)

Cut into slices 1 lb. of liver, put in a greased dripping tin covered with a layer of brown crumbs; leave a small space between the slices. Make a stuffing of 3 tablespoonfuls of breadcrumbs, 1 teaspoonful of chopped parsley, ½ teaspoonful of sweet herbs (if liked), and a seasoning of pepper and salt; mix with a little milk into a stiff paste, or use onion stuffing; place a thin layer over each piece of liver, and a slice of thin bacon on the top. Pour round a little stock or water, and bake slowly for about 1 hour. To serve, arrange the slices in a circle on a dish, thicken the gravy, add a dessertspoonful of Worcester sauce, and pour round the meat.

HEART (STEWED)

One ox heart or 2 sheep's hearts, cut open, stuff with forcemeat or sage and onions, cover up well with fat bacon and tie round with tape, dust with flour, place in a dish with water or stock and cover over tightly and bake about 3 hours; baste frequently. Serve with rich gravy.

Or it may be stuffed, wrapped in bacon, and put in a very well-greased paper bag; for a short time before serving take off the paper to get it brown.

HEAD & BRAIN
RECIPES

SHEEP'S HEAD TO MAKE
FOUR GOOD DISHES

(1) SCOTCH BARLEY BROTH (enough for 6 or 7 people).–Split the head, remove the tongue and brains, and lay them aside. Wash the head well, and soak all night in 2½ quarts of water, with a tablespoonful of salt. Next morning put the head and the water in which it has been soaking in a pot with 6 ozs. of washed barley, and cook gently 2 hours. Add 2 turnips, 2 carrots, 2 onions (or 1 leek), all sliced, a little parsley, pepper, and salt, and simmer 1 hour. Take meat off the bones, cut up small, put back in the pot, and reheat before serving.

(2) THE BRAINS make a light and nourishing meal for an invalid if poached in a little of the broth, and served with white sauce, or they can be shaped into flat cakes and dipped in batter and fried (brain fritters). Or cook in scallop shells or a pie-dish with some well-flavoured brown gravy or tomato sauce, and a sprinkling of breadcrumbs on the top. They should always be blanched (boiling water poured over them) before cooking.

(3) **THE BONES** should be boiled again to make soup.

(4) **THE TONGUE** will make a very good supper dish for 2 people. Cut it in half, lengthwise, and place in a small stoneware pot with a piece of dripping or butter (walnut size), a tiny bunch of mixed herbs, and some flavouring, such as peppercorns, mace, pepper, and salt (very little of each), and a few bits of vegetables sliced up if these are handy. Pour a gill of the sheep's head or any other broth over it (or water) and stew gently for 1½ hours. Then add 2 ozs. of cooked rice or small macaroni, and simmer for 1 hour more. Serve in the pot.

BRAIN CAKES (ENTRÉE)

Remove brains from sheep's head, wash in cold vinegar and water. Put into boiling water for 10 minutes, drain; beat lightly with a fork in a basin, 1 tablespoonful chopped parsley, ½ teaspoonful of salt, ¼ teaspoonful of pepper, and 2 tablespoonfuls of breadcrumbs, add 1 egg. Have ready some boiling fat, dip in fat an iron spoon, take up a small portion of the mixture, and drop into the fat. If too light it will puff up, so add more breadcrumbs; then cook remainder from 3 to 5 minutes, drain on soft paper. Serve on toast.

SHEEP'S HEAD PIE

1 sheep's head
¼ lb. pearl barley
2 ozs. lean ham
1 or 2 hard-boiled eggs
1 tablespoonful chopped parsley
½ teaspoonful salt
¼ teaspoonful pepper
½ pint stock that the head was boiled in

for the pastry
½ lb. flour
¼ lb. dripping or lard
Level teaspoonful of baking powder
Little cold water
Pinch of salt

Cut the dripping or lard with a knife into inch pieces, drop into the flour, add water by degrees, knead lightly with the fingers, roll out. Divide baking powder into 3 parts; sprinkle one part of the pastry, fold both ends over into the middle, press down all round with tips of floured fingers. Roll again, and repeat process twice; put it aside, if possible, for ½ hour before using. Wet edges of pie-dish with water or egg, place a narrow strip on them, and press the inside edge well down. Put in the meat, seasoning, and eggs cut in slices; wet the edges of the pastry and lay on the top; gently press and pare the edges tidy, using them to make leaves and a rose for decoration. Be sure to prick a hole in the centre, or better at the side of the rose, if one is made. Boil the head, after washing it well in warm water containing salt; at least 3 lots of water should be used. Wash the barley, put into the pan with the head, and boil 3 hours. Remove meat carefully, skin the tongue, and cut it in small slices. Place in the dish in layers with slices of egg and ham, meat, and tongue; moisten with the stock.

N.B.—Save remainder of stock to make Sheep's Broth.

CALF'S HEAD (BOILED)

Clean the half or whole of a calf's head, then by means of a small pointed knife remove all the bones, and also the brains. When this is done, roll up the head lengthwise in the form of a galantine, then fasten it up in a clean buttered cloth, and bind it with a piece of tape to keep it in a good shape. Put it in a saucepan with enough cold water to cover it, 1 tablespoonful of salt, and a good plateful of raw vegetables; bring to the boil, then skim, and cover the pan over with the lid and let it continue boiling for 3½ hours according to size. Take it up and remove the cloth, place the head on a hot dish, and serve over it good parsley sauce, in which put the calf's brains, previously blanched and cut up in little dice shapes; crimp the ear by cutting it with the scissors, skin the tongue, and arrange on the side by the head, and serve very hot.

BRAWN (COW)

1 cow-heel
½ lb. cooked ham
1 teaspoonful Lemco
Black pepper, grate of nutmeg
2 dessertspoonfuls sweet herbs and parsley

Cut ham and cow-heel into pieces, stew in a little water with Lemco; when nearly done add herbs, etc. Press into a wet mould. Turn out when cold. Stew 4 hours or longer.

BRAWN (PIG)

Split in pieces a pig's head, salt well all over, remove eyes, put brains on a dish, and salt them; keep the head in salt for 4 days or a week, rubbing it occasionally; wash in several waters to remove salt, place in a stew-jar covered with cold water and a lid, get it to boil, and simmer till meat is tender and will leave the bones, about 3-4 hours. Remove from liquor and take out the bones, cut meat in fine pieces. Put into a deep brawn tin with holes in the bottom, put on a weight about 4 lbs. to press it. Next day remove out of the tin, cut in pieces again, put in a pan, and take some of the previous day's jelly (with fat removed); bring to a boil, add a good amount of pepper, 2 ozs. at the least. Keep the tongue whole, and place in lengthway into each mould, surrounded by the mixture; let them cool.

SAVOURY JELLIES

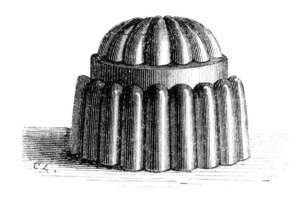

FISH JELLY

Boil ¾lb. fish bones with a sliced onion, few peppercorns and allspice, teaspoonful salt, ½ cup vinegar, a tablespoonful mixed herbs, shell and the white of an egg, and liberal pint of water; boil ½ hour; dissolve in it is 1½ ozs. of leaf gelatine. Put through a fine sieve into a wet mould.

JELLY PIE

1 lb. raw lean beef
2 or 3 rashers bacon
Chopped parsley
2 hard-boiled eggs
Pepper and salt

Arrange in fireproof dish, pour over some vegetable stock; cover and cook gently 3 hours. Let it cool; remove fat off the top, stir in ½ oz. dissolved gelatine to pint of stock; pour over and cool. Serve cold with salad.

N.B.—If liked, it may be used as a mould with alternate layers of any left-over cooked vegetables cut in slices.

JELLY (CALF'S FOOT)

Chop 2 nicely cleaned calf's feet small; place in a stew-pan covered with water; bring to a boil; remove pieces, wash them, throw away the water and rinse the pan; replace and cover with 5 pints of cold water; simmer for 5 hours and skim frequently; strain the stock and let it cool. When cold and set, remove the fat and wipe jelly with a clean cloth. Place it in a pan with the whites and shells of 2 eggs, 4 ozs. loaf sugar, and a bay leaf. Whisk till it boils; cover, and let it form a crust; strain through a jelly bag 2 or 3 times till clear; add a wineglass of sherry and ½ wineglass of brandy.

JELLY (SWEET) (COW-HEEL)

1 cow-heel
(ask butcher for one underboiled)
3 pints water
Sugar to taste
Whites and shells of 2 eggs
3 wineglassfuls sherry

Put heel into pan with water, boil gently till
reduced to 1 pint; strain, and let it go cold;
remove all fat. Place in a pan with sugar, the
whites and shells of eggs; beat well, add
wine; let it boil about 1 minute, draw off the
fire, let it stand a few minutes, strain through
a jelly bag or very fine muslin.

FRUITS
OF THE SEA

CONGER EEL (DRESSED)

2 lbs. cut of eel
¼ teaspoonful mixed herbs
3 tablespoonfuls golden brown crumbs
Pepper, salt, cayenne
1 oz. butter or dripping
1 egg
½ lemon rind, grated (if liked)

Skin eel, brush over with beaten egg, roll in mixed herbs and seasonings. Put in greased dish, with butter in pieces on top; baste a few times. Bake 2-3 hours.

CONGER EEL (BAKED)

Place eel in a stew-dish, season with pepper and salt, put on top a few pieces of butter or dripping, nearly cover with milk. Place a cover over it, bake about 2 hours, basting occasionally. Cover dish with a frill and serve hot.

EEL PIE

1 lb. cold eel, free from bones and skin
½ lb. mashed potatoes
Pepper and salt
1 oz. flour
½ pint milk

Put eel into well-greased dish, add
seasonings, chopped parsley (if liked); make
a sauce of flour and milk, and pour over fish.
Cover with potatoes mashed with milk and
butter, ruffle top with fork; bake 1 hour.
Decorate with parsley.

EEL PUDDING

1 lb. cooked eel
1 lb. mashed potatoes
1 oz. dripping
1 gill milk or fish stock
1 dried egg
Little anchovy sauce
Pepper and salt
Few chopped capers (if desired)

Grease a pie-dish or basin, sprinkle with browned crumbs. Remove skin and bones from eel, chop it, mix with potatoes, and warmed dripping, add other ingredients. Place in dish. Bake 1 hour or steam 1½ hours. Turn out, serve with egg or parsley sauce.

RED HERRINGS

Place them in a deep jug, and cover with boiling water; remove in 3 minutes, and serve at once. This prevents a disagreeable smell in the house, and also refines the flavour.

Or immerse in hot water for 2 minutes, wipe dry, smear inside with butter, grill or fry for 5 minutes.

HERRINGS (POTTED)

Eight herrings. Clean and remove the backbones, cut off heads and fins, wipe dry; sprinkle insides with little pepper and salt. Put a layer in bottom of dish, heads and tails reversed, or if preferred make into rolls. Cut 3 small onions into rings, put some on top of the fish, with 2 bay leaves, little thyme, sage, and parsley. Mix in a cup ½ teaspoonful of salt, ½ teaspoonful of pepper, 1 teaspoonful of mustard, ½ teaspoonful mixed spice, and a tablespoonful of olive-oil. Mix well together, add ¼ cup of vinegar or stout, gradually. Cover dish; bake in sharp oven 40 minutes. Can be served hot or cold.

HERRINGS (SOUSED)

4 to 6 fresh herrings
12 peppercorns
¼ teaspoonful salt
1 blade mace
1 gill vinegar
½ gill water

Take out the backbones, roll up the fish or put them in a dish head and tail, pour the mixture over, and bake 30 minutes. Serve cold.

MEATLESS DISHES

PICKLED BRITISH SPROUTS

1 lb. British sprouts
1 pint vinegar
½d. packet of mixed spice

Trim and put into salted water for 24 hours, drain in a colander. Boil vinegar, pour over sprouts, add the spice, put in a jar or bottle, tie down. Keep 2 weeks before using.

PARSNIP PIE

Two good-sized parsnips, cut up small, cover with half milk and half water, season with pepper and salt; simmer till tender; strain off liquor into a basin, put parsnips into a pie-dish. Make a cheese sauce with a piece of margarine size of walnut, melt in a pan, stir in nearly 1 tablespoonful of flour, add gradually some of the liquor, and stir to keep smooth; add some grated cheese, stir till it melts, pour over the parsnips. Bake and brown in the oven.

NETTLES (BOILED)

Place very well washed nettles in a little water, boil till thick, drain if necessary, mix with evaporated milk, pepper, and salt.

N.B.—A valuable food for consumptives.

NETTLES AS A VEGETABLE

Nettles, when gathered young, make a wholesome and delicious dish, much resembling spinach. Cut the tops of the nettles only, pick over carefully, to free from any grass, etc., and wash well. Boil 15 or 20 minutes; then lift out the nettles, drain, chop, and, if possible, rub through a wire sieve. Return to the empty pan with about 2 ozs. of butter or a tablespoonful of cream. Make thoroughly hot, and serve at once, on toast.

The larger leaves and stalks of the nettles can be used to make nettle beer.

SPINACH AND EGGS AU GRATIN

Boil and strain 4 lbs. spinach for 4 or 6 persons, reheat with 1 oz. butter, ¼ oz. salt, a tablespoonful milk or water. Beat up 2 eggs, stir into ½ pint hot milk and add 4 tablespoonfuls grated cheese, stir till it thickens, do not let it boil. Place spinach on a dish, pour over the egg sauce and brown under grill.

CHEESE PUDDING

4 ozs. bread crumbs
1 oz. butter
3 ozs. cheese
1 pint milk
2 eggs
Salt to taste

Put the bread crumbs and cheese into a well
buttered dish. Add the boiling milk and then
the yolks of the eggs. Beat the whites to a
stiff froth and stir in last of all. Bake for half
an hour in a moderate oven.

CABBAGE MOULD

1 lb. cooked potatoes
1 cold cooked cabbage
½ oz. butter
½ teaspoonful salt
½ teaspoonful pepper
1 tablespoonful breadcrumbs

Grease a mould, line it with breadcrumbs;
press all lumps out of potatoes, cut cabbage
very small, add seasonings, press in mould.
Bake ¼ hour.

TASTY TREATS

TRIPE AND ONIONS

1 lb. tripe
3 middle-sized onions
½ pint milk
1 oz. flour
Salt
Pepper

Stew onions, tripe, and milk together about ½ hour or till tender; remove tripe on to hot dish. Thicken milk with flour, pour over tripe. Serve hot.

N.B.—The time for cooking varies according to the way it has been prepared by the dealer in different districts, sometimes it has been parboiled, sometimes not.

PIG'S TROTTERS

4 trotters
2 ozs. dripping
1 sprig parsley
Pepper and salt
½ pint brown gravy
1 teaspoonful vinegar
Breadcrumbs, about 2 tablespoonfuls
1½ ozs. grated cheese

Boil till tender, remove bones; fry onion cut in slices, brown in dripping; stew for ½ hour. Make forcemeat of crumbs, parsley, seasoning, and little gravy; place this in the cavities caused by removing bones; lay in a pie-dish, cover with a few crumbs, onions, vinegar, and gravy; sprinkle with grated cheese, brown, and serve in the dish as it is.

TESTICLE SCALLOPS

Mince some cold sheep testicles, and season them. Butter a pudding dish, and put in a layer of the mince and next a layer of breadcrumbs till the dish is full, place on this a little butter, and moisten with milk; pour gravy with a little lemon juice over the top, and bake for ½ hour.

MUTTON CUSTARD

Two ozs. mutton kidney suet, 1 pint new milk. Shred suet very fine; put with milk in a 2-lb. jam jar, place in a tin of water in hot oven till reduced to half. Strain through fine muslin. When put the milk into the oven with a very little sugar and lemon rind (if liked); leave to get hot; remove and let cool, and take off the fat again. Give to child very hot. It is good for a cough taken just before going to sleep, and is also good for dysentery if mixed with 2 teaspoonfuls of cornflour and a teaspoonful taken every 2 hours.

CABBAGE FARCE

1 firm white cabbage
Sausage meat or cold meat (minced)

Cut away all the hard leaves, wash the cabbage, put into boiling water with salt and parboil it. Drain, cut in halves, and spread with the meat well seasoned. Tie together and bake in lard in a dripping tin, with sliced tomatoes on top, till tender.

SEMOLINA PATTIES

Make into pastry:

      1 lb. mashed potatoes

      3 ozs. flour

      1½ ozs. melted dripping

      1 dried egg, salt

Roll out pastry and cut into rounds for each tin.

      1 pint milk and stock mixed

      2 ozs. semolina

      2 ozs. grated cheese

      Whole tomato or sauce

      ½ oz. chopped onion, or

      ¼ oz. onion powder

      1 tablespoonful chopped parsley

For the filling, boil the milk, stock, and onion together till onion is soft; sprinkle in carefully the semolina. Stir till it is thick and smooth, add chopped tomato, parsley, and other ingredients; mix well, cool a little, and put into the pastry, wet edges, put on the top pastry, and bake about ½ hour.

SEMOLINA RISSOLES

4 ozs. semolina
3 ozs. grated cheese
½ teaspoonful English mustard
1 pint milk
1 egg
Salt and pepper

Bring milk to the boil, shake in carefully the semolina, stirring well; simmer till cooked; add the cheese, seasonings, and lastly beaten egg. Put to cool, then shape into rissoles, adding if necessary very little flour to stiffen; dip in browned crumbs. Fry in a basket.

OX CHEEK

Soak the head in cold water for 2 hours; take out the bones first.

At night put on it ¼ lb. Demerara sugar and 2 ozs. saltpetre; the next morning add ½ lb. of common salt. Let it remain in the brine 4 days, turning it every morning. Boil 7 hours, then press in a tongue tin.

MEAT GÂTEAU

½ lb. cold meat, minced
¼ lb. fine breadcrumbs
¼ teaspoonful salt
1 saltspoonful pepper
½ teaspoonful mixed herbs
3 ozs. suet (less if meat is fat)
2 eggs
A little stock
A tiny grate of nutmeg

Mix together, put in greased basin decorated with slices of hard-boiled egg; steam 1¼ hours. Serve with brown gravy poured round it.

BEVERAGES

BEEF TEA (RAW)

½ lb. lean neck of beef
Pinch salt
Little water

Cut beef into strips, shred it, place in a jar with salt, add water to cover the meat. Cover, allow it to stand 2 or more hours, pass through a coarse sieve, press well, and get all the juice out. Serve in a coloured glass.

PARSNIP WINE

¼ oz. yeast
2 gallons water
½ peck parsnips
7 lbs. loaf sugar

Scrub parsnips and boil until quite tender.
Strain on to sugar, stir in yeast, leave
24 hours. Skim, strain, and bottle, do not
cork for 3 days, then not tightly.

*N.B.—Test for sweetness — put an egg into wine,
and if sweet enough egg will easily float.*

NETTLE BEER

2 lbs. Nettles
Handful dandelion
½ oz. yeast
2 quarts water
Brown sugar to taste

Wash herbs, put into a pan with sufficient water to cover; boil about 20 minutes, strain, sweeten; if too strong, dilute with cold water. When almost cold add the yeast; let it "work" about 3 hours; when all has risen, skim off top. Put into dry, screw-topped bottles, and leave 24 hours before using. Keep in a cool place.

N.B.—Should be made when nettles are young.

DESSERT

CUSTARD (JELLIES)

1 pint custard
3 ozs. ripe fruit
¾ oz. gelatine
Sugar or golden syrup to taste

Dissolve gelatine in 3 tablespoonfuls of hot water; add it to the hot custard; stir fruit in, sweetening; add all together and pour in a wet mould or deep dish. Let it set.

CUSTARD PUDDING

1 pint milk
2 eggs
1 tablespoonful sugar

Whisk eggs, stir with the milk and sugar, put in buttered pie-dish. Bake 20 minutes, or steam in a buttered mould 35 minutes.

ILKLEY PUDDING

1½ ozs. butter

3½ ozs. sugar

3½ ozs. flour

3 tablespoonsful baking powder

2 eggs

3 tablespoonsful milk

Steam three-quarters of an hour.

PATRIOTIC PUDDING

8 ozs. flour

1½ teaspoonful baking powder

3 ozs. sugar

4 ozs. butter

a little milk

2 eggs

Artisanal Jam

Cream the butter, and add sugar, flour, and eggs, well beaten. Lastly add the baking powder. Put a little jam into the bottom of the mould, then pour in the pudding and steam for one hour.

VINEGAR CAKE

1 lb. flour
½ lb. sugar
½ lb. currants
6 ozs. butter
Seasoning to taste
1 small teaspoonful of soda
(dissolved in warm milk to make it the
consistency of plum cake)

Add one tablespoonful of vinegar the last
thing, bake two hours.

MILK JELLY

1 oz. leaf gelatine
1 pint water
¾ lb. loaf sugar
1 pint milk
1 egg

Soak the gelatine in half pint water overnight. Then add the other half pint boiling water and stir. Put the loaf sugar into a bowl and pour over it the boiling milk, stir till dissolved, then add the gelatine, etc., and lastly a beaten-up egg. Set in a mould.

BLANCMANGE

1 oz. powdered gelatine
4 ozs. powdered sugar
1 quart milk

Warm the milk gently with the gelatine and sugar, and stir till all is dissolved. Pour into a mould and allow to set.

BLANCMANGE SPONGE

2 pints milk

2½ ozs. of cornflour

3 eggs

2 ozs. sugar

Boil milk and cornflour for 10 minutes; remove from fire. Beat whites of eggs very stiff, and put aside. Beat the yolks with the sugar, and stir into the cornflour. Mix in the whites lightly, and cook for 1 minute. Put into a wet mould.

SEMOLINA PUDDING (1)

4 ozs. flour
2 ozs. semolina
½ teaspoonful baking powder
Jam to line basin
Milk or milk and water to mix

Make into a soft dough, grease a basin, line
with jam. Put in dough, cover with greased
paper. Steam 2 hours.

SEMOLINA PUDDING (2)

2 ozs. ground rice
1 pint milk, salt
1 or 2 eggs
1 oz. sugar

Boil the milk, sugar, and rice for 10 minutes, stirring all the time; then add the beaten eggs. Place in a fancy dish and cover with a layer of apricot jam. Decorate with chopped burnt almonds and some whipped cream.

N.B.—Very good, hot or cold.

SEMOLINA PUDDING (3)

2 ozs. semolina
1 oz. sugar
1 pint milk
1 egg
Flavouring to taste
Pinch of salt

Blend the semolina with a little cold milk.
Boil remainder of milk with flavouring, pour
on to the semolina, sweeten, return to pan,
and cook about 15 minutes. Cool a little,
then add the egg yolk, and fold in carefully
the white, which has been beaten to a stiff
froth. Pour into a greased pie-dish, and bake
in a hot oven ½ hour.

SEMOLINA PUDDING (4)

1½ pints milk
2 eggs
2 tablespoonsful semolina
1 tablespoonful sugar
Flavouring

Mix the semolina with cold milk and boil up the rest. Add the yolks of the eggs to the semolina, pour over it the boiling milk and stir well. Put back into the pan, bring to boiling point, then add the beaten whites, sugar, and flavour. Bake in a buttered dish half an hour.

SEMOLINA BLANCMANGE

2 ozs. semolina
1½ pints milk
1 level tablespoonful castor sugar

Put milk on to heat for 5 minutes, gradually sift in the semolina. Stir about 15 minutes and add sugar. Put into a wet 1½ pint earthenware mould, and stand in cold water. Can be served with any fruit sauce, stewed fruit, or custard sauce. If necessary it will do made with half water and half milk.

About the Author

Graham Hughes is a British adventurer, filmmaker, writer and presenter from Liverpool, England.

Between 2009 and 2013 he used his (then) incredibly powerful UK passport to visit every country in the world without flying, setting a new Guinness World Record™.

In 2014 he moved to Panama and lived off-grid on an island he won on an American survivalist TV show.

However, during that time, his beloved country was overrun by vicious idiots who, instead of building a better future for their children, are obsessed with dragging the nation back to some infantised version of the past: the days of rationing, recession, and rickets.

Hughes returned to the UK in 2017 to try to help people understand the consequences of their cruel and thoughtless actions. As far as he was concerned, if we forged ahead with Brexit, the UK's days as an important world power were well and truly numbered.

He was the creator of the *Three Blokes In A Pub* podcast and helped organize a number of major anti-Brexit demonstrations across the UK.

However, his calls for decency and common sense fell on deaf ears as, being a scouser, he didn't sound posh enough for people to take seriously.

C'est la vie.

Printed in Great Britain
by Amazon